Calm Trader:

Win in the Stock Market
Without Losing Your Mind

By Steve Burns & Holly Burns

Contents

Harness your emotions, and the rest will come.

Anyone who has been following my Twitter account, or my NewTraderU.com blog knows that I believe that a trader must learn to control their emotions in order to be successful. I don't want to make it sound like I think this is easy, or that I haven't had my own challenges along the way. On the contrary, I struggled as a new trader, just like everyone else. I have learned some important truths about the benefits of staying calm that have helped me both mentally and emotionally, and made me a successful trader and investor for more than 20 years.

I haven't learned these truths alone. I have had the help of my talented wife, who in addition to being a web developer and professional writer, has also been a licensed massage therapist, stress management consultant, and meditation instructor for more than ten years. Since entering my world, she has witnessed many traders affected by the same issues that she has helped professional athletes, performers, and other business professionals overcome. I'm lucky to have her guidance and support.

I hope that these principles will help propel you to more trading success, and that you will find happiness in every aspect of your life.

-Steve and Holly Burns
www.NewTraderU.com
@sjosephburns
@hollyannburns

Introduction

The stock market is a device for transferring money from the IMPATIENT *to the patient.* – Warren Buffett

In the financial markets the calm trader is usually the winning trader. There is an advantage to keeping your emotions in check when everyone else around you is losing their mind. It's difficult for bad traders to stay calm, because their lack of knowledge and confidence negatively impact their trading. It's a catch 22 that never ends. They lack confidence because they are trading their own opinions rather than quantifiable facts, but it's difficult to have faith in their trading abilities when they have no real trading system.

A trader needs support and structure to stay calm and feel confident. By developing a detailed trading methodology, writing a trading plan, and implementing hard and fast risk management and position sizing rules, a trader will gain the peace of mind necessary to give them an edge in the markets.

Most studies put the survival rate of traders at about 10%. What are they doing wrong?

-Trading with real money before they have educated themselves
-Trading too big and risking too much at any one time
-Not having enough money to trade effectively
-Predicting what will happen instead of trading what is happening
-Wanting to get rich quick

The overarching theme is the inability to stay calm and wait. Instead, of rushing in and hoping for the best, a trader should strive to be patient and trade in the moment.

-Wait until you are ready to trade a quantified system with a written plan
-Be calm, trade small, and build your account safely over time
-Don't stress yourself by trading with a small account that is unable to manage commission costs and slippage
-Calmly trade the price action that is happening and not what you want to happen
-Choose to get rich over time by using sound trading practices instead of going broke quickly because of poor risk management techniques

In trading, the biggest obstacle to our success is our own fear, greed, ego, and opinions. The ability to trade calmly by following your system is a skill few traders ever develop. This book will give you the principles to trade calmly, and the tools to overcome stressful trading situations.

If you follow these principles, your trading will become profitable because you will be able to stand outside the market's emotional mood swings and observe the price action as a detached witness. You will be able to make your decisions for entries and exits based on signals that put the odds in your favor.

You will have an edge over traders who are being swept away by their emotions. You will make money following trends while others are fighting them. You will have the confidence to buy during a moment of maximum fear while others are selling for a loss. You will be profitable by controlling your emotions and trading based on quantifiable facts.

This book pinpoints the fourteen areas that lead to panicked trading and failure, and practical exercises to help you in times of stress. By managing your emotions, following your trading plan, and staying calm when things don't go as planned, you will become a better trader and a happier person.

You will be a calm trader.

I think investment psychology is by far the more important element, followed by risk control, with the least important consideration being the question of where you buy and sell. – Tom Basso

The financial markets are unpredictable. Unexpected events commonly occur, while the sure thing rarely happens. The best time to buy low is typically when maximum fear is present and traders think the end of the world is near.

A trader or investor can have an ideal buy price target in mind, based on either a chart price support level or a fundamental valuation, but when the price actually drops to their desired range, the fear of another drop may stop them from following their plan. Instead, they freeze and are unable to act as price comes and goes. Regardless of whether they are proven right in the long run, they are unable to take advantage of an opportunity because of their uncontrolled emotions.

The best dip buying opportunity or good risk/reward ratio setup usually comes from fear and irrational panic in the markets. The energy and velocity of the fear forces prices down to desirable buy points, but traders and investors are often unable to jump in due to the fear of a continued slide in prices. Ultimately, emotions cost traders a lot of money.

Here is an example of how uncontrolled emotional errors can influence growth stock investors, trend traders, and momentum traders.

The initial plan for this group is to buy high and sell higher. A growth stock could be in a $95 to $100 trading range for months, and they decide to buy if it breaks out over $100 in the hopes that it will go higher if that price resistance is overcome. But when price gaps up and opens at $102 they don't buy. Instead, they decide to wait for it to pull back to at least $101 or even $100.

The next day it opens at $103 and continues to go up to $104. The fear of buying higher made the trader wait for a pullback that never came, and miss the breakout they were given. The inability to follow their own trading plan cost them money because they were unable to make adjustments and capitalize on opportunity.

The above example is not uncommon. The inability to stay calm and follow a prewritten trading plan in real-time is what trips up most traders. When emotions overcome your ability to follow your plan, you have gone from a calm trader to one that is emotionally reactionary. Instead of basing decisions on emotions, base them *only* on quantifiable price action. Developing a winning trading system that fits your personality and comfort level is crucial to your success, and creating a trading plan that you can believe in is imperative. Developing a trading plan that keeps you as stress-free as possible should be your number one priority before you make your first trade.

Without the right mindset, you will not be able to weather the setbacks, draw downs, and market volatility, and you will eventually give up on your trading journey.

Exercise: Spend time developing a trading plan that you feel comfortable using, and that you can actually follow. It will take time and dedication to create a successful plan, but it will eliminate much of the stress involved with trading, and make you profitable in the long run.

Components of a trading plan:

-When to enter a trade
-When to exit a trade
-Stop placement
-Position sizing
-Money management parameters
-What to trade
-Trading time frames
-Backtesting results
-Performance review
-Risk vs. reward

Mindfulness over markets

If instead of saying, "I'm going to do this trade," you say, "I'm going to watch myself do this trade," all of a sudden you find that the process is a lot easier. – Jack D. Schwager, The New Market Wizards: Conversations with America's Top Traders

Too many traders sit down at their trading desks and are overcome by the emotional rollercoaster of risk and reward. Instead of trading what is happening in the markets, they are focused on the money, basing their trades on how much they can win or lose. Instead, they should be focused on the price action and the market's movements.

You will experience a lot of anxiety if you spend your time watching your equity curve minute by minute, agonizing over what will happen next. A trader must create emotional distance from the market's feedback loop of profits and losses. The difference in trading the markets with real money versus watching the price action from a detached perspective with no skin in the game, is like watching a sporting event versus playing in the game yourself.

Your stress is higher based on how much is at stake at any given time. Like an athlete, a trader may be great in practice but then choke when it's time to make the winning move. Being a professional is about the ability to use your talent at the right moment. And while stress is always present, and can even be a motivator at the right levels, how you manage that stress will be the difference between success and failure.
Traders who don't follow their trading plan suffer losses because they are unaware of their feelings during losses, large wins, or volatility in their account equity.

Most the time our fears are unfounded, but they also may be trying to protect us from a dangerous situation. It's up to us to determine if our thoughts are coming from a trusted source, or if they are being hijacked by our emotions. The only way to determine this is to become mindful; to step back from our own thoughts and observe them without judgement.

Mindfulness means that you have a higher level of awareness. You observe your own emotions, thoughts, and circumstances without any emotional prejudice. A person that is mindful is concerned with what is happening around them, and filters their actions through logic, reason, and the goals they want to achieve.

In contrast, emotional behavior is fueled by strong emotions that lead to uncontrolled impulses that don't align with a plan or goal. Without being tested with mindfulness, emotions can lead us astray, and can definitely cost a trader money. It's important that you learn to step back from your thought process and filter everything through the eyes of an unbiased observer. Only then will you be able to see if what you are feeling is an uncontrolled emotion like greed, ego, or fear, or whether it should be acted on logically.

A trader can make a quantum leap in their results when they transition from emotions controlling their behavior and embrace the power that comes from self-awareness.

Exercise: One of the best ways to keep track of your feelings is by keeping a trading journal every day. A trading journal is a tool that teaches the trader about themselves. It's like your diary for your relationship with the financial markets. This will help you keep a visual record that you can refer to on your trading journey.

Things to ask yourself:

-How do I feel today? Nervous? Excited?
-What is my emotion trying to tell me?
-What is this emotion based on?
-Is it trying to keep me safe from something? What?
-Is it a legitimate emotion or based on a false premise?
-How would I feel if I decided to ignore this emotion?
-How would I feel if I decided not to trade today based on this emotion?

Be mindful of your current state of emotions at any given time. Know whether you are happy, sad, angry, lonely, or stressed out. Do a self-checkup every day before you trade. Write your emotional state in your trading journal before you start trading, and make a commitment to be more mindful of our feelings.

Trend following is a form of technical analysis. However, it's not predictive technical analysis, but rather it's reactive technical analysis. This is key to understand. – Michael Covel

All that should matter to a trader is what they are doing right now, in the current moment; their potential entry setups, their stop losses, and what they are doing with their open positions. A trader has to focus on what's happening, not what they want to happen or hope will happen next. The past is over and the future doesn't exist yet. All we can do is focus on the present moment.

A trader experiences stress because emotions intrude on their logical thought process. When times are challenging, fear and regret can cloud their thinking. No amount of regret brings back lost money, and it's a waste of energy and time. Learn from past mistakes and accept them as life lessons. Sometimes the lessons are expensive, but they will prove to be valuable in the end. Learn from them and adopt them as rules in your trading plan so you can grow as a trader and minimize future mistakes.

No matter how much you want to believe that you can forecast the future, you can't. Accurate predictions are not possible because the future hasn't happened, and the universe is unpredictable. If you are accurate when you predict a certain outcome, acknowledge that it's a coincidence and nothing else. Focus on trading the present price action, and react to how it's performing based on quantified methodology.

Backtesting of price history and price targets for projected trends have their limitations. The present price action is constantly evolving, despite previous patterns or future potential. It's possible to study price history to observe emotional and technical trading patterns, and you can set potential targets to previous support or resistance on charts to give you the probabilities of success. However, the key to trading profitably is not found in the backtests or the chart pattern projections. Successful trading comes from the process that you adopt for entries, exits and position sizing. Flow with current price action to capture trends, cut losses, and take trades with great risk/reward ratios.

There are two aspects of trading in the now. The first is to react to price action as it occurs in the present moment, taking entry signals without trying to predict what will happen next. When you enter a trade, you don't know if your stop loss will be hit first, or your trailing stop will trigger after a long and profitable trade. Your profitability lies in your flexibility to follow the price.

The second part of trading in the now is practicing mindfulness with a focus on identifying your feelings, thoughts, and how they can affect your ability to make the right decisions in entries, exits, and position sizing. The ability to do the right thing at the right moment is all that matters. Emotional time travel to the past or future is a dangerous practice. In trading, this detrimental habit will feed the emotions of regret and dread, and it will eventually be mentally and financially draining. Learn to manage your emotions and trade based on the right signals, position sizing, and trade management system, and you will effectively execute your trading plan in the now.

Exercise:

Before you begin to trade, practice this exercise to make sure you are in the moment. Wherever you are when you trade, notice what you are experiencing around you right now through the senses of sound, touch, smell, and sight.

-Take a deep breath, close your eyes, and exhale. What three things can you hear? Is there a car passing by, the sound of a ticking clock, your own breathing? Spend a few seconds with each sound.
-Take another deep breath, and exhale. What can you feel? The chair you are sitting in, the breeze from a window, your wallet? Spend a few seconds with each thing you can feel.
-Take another deep breath, and exhale. What can you smell? The smell of coffee, freshly mowed grass, breakfast? Spend a few seconds with each smell.
-Now open your eyes, take another deep breath, and exhale. What do you see around you? Another person, your desk, a pet? Spend a few seconds with each thing you see.

This exercise is meant to bring you into the present moment. It's also a great way to relax enough to notice if you feel any tension in your body. Practicing this exercise before every trade will take less than a minute, and it will help you become more self-aware.

The art of self-control

It's hard enough to know what the market is going to do; if you don't know what you are going to do, the game is lost. – Alexander Elder, The New Trading for a Living.

In the late 1960s and early 1970s, studies by Stanford University demonstrated that being patient and exercising self-control are important factors in our success and happiness[1]. The researchers performed tests in delayed gratification by giving children a choice between an immediate reward like a marshmallow, cookie, or pretzel or waiting for 15 minutes and getting two rewards.

Stanford researchers found that children who were able to wait and not eat the initial treat and receive the additional reward, went on to be more successful in life. They had higher SAT scores, better educational achievement, and lower body mass index scores. This study shows the power of impulse control. If you pass on immediate gratification and exercise self-control, you will likely experience a larger reward in the future.

For traders, this equates to letting a winner run rather than cutting a winner short for no reason. Giving up the small win gives you a larger win later in a trending market. This principle can also apply to taking a small loss when you are proven wrong, even if you don't want to. Most traders don't want to take a loss and make it real because they want to give it a chance to recover. The downside is that you can get caught on the wrong side of a market, and end up with a huge loss. Self-control means doing what you need to do, even when you don't want to do it.

The inability to control our impulses and need for immediate gratification can lead to violence and addiction, and is the undoing of many people. In trading, the lack of impulse control makes traders take large positions in a desperate attempt to get back big losses, or spend money and time on someone who promises to give them the secret of wealth creation. The impulse to get rich quickly is usually followed by the disappointment of losing a lot of money. Making money in the financial markets comes from researching and following a detailed trading plan and system.

The ability to control your impulse to get rich quick, gives you the discipline and focus to study the markets when you would rather be doing something else. The hours of education required to be a successful trader are long and hard. There are many more exciting things that a trader could be doing on a Friday night instead of reading about entry signals. But dedicating time to your trading studies is necessary to your successful career, and it will make you a better and more disciplined trader.

---

[1] J Pers Soc Psychol. 1972 Feb; 21(2):204-18.

Cognitive and attentional mechanisms in delay of gratification.

Mischel W, Ebbesen EB, Zeiss AR.

You need to save enough to accumulate a good sized trading account. Saving is a lot less fun than taking vacations or buying expensive new cars. For some, this is not an issue. They either have self-control naturally, or they were raised by parents who taught them delayed gratification. For others, this will be the most difficult part of their trading journey. The simple fact is that you must have a trading account with enough money to trade comfortably, both mentally and financially. And unless you receive a windfall, you will need to earn and save your trading capital.

The best way to help yourself control your impulses is by having clearly defined goals and a vision of what you want your future to look like. When you experience an overwhelming desire to do something that could be detrimental to your plan, you can look at it through the filter of whether it's moving you toward your goals or away from them. This technique will help you find a space in your thoughts between your impulses and your long term goals. It will keep you from following the wrong path and jeopardizing the big picture.

When impulses aren't controlled, people trade their goals and future gains for their immediate desires. This is a terrible trade. The best way to implement impulse control as a trader is to have a clear set of goals and a detailed trading plan that you follow religiously. In the financial markets, money is transferred from those who can't control their impulses to those who can.

Exercise:
Create a detailed life plan. Just like your trading plan, it should expound on your goals and how you will reach them.

Ask yourself these questions:

-Where do you want to be in the next five, ten, twenty, and fifty years?
-What age do you want to retire?
-Where do you want to live when you retire?
-How do you envision helping those around you?
-Do you want to own a home or travel the world?
-What do you see yourself doing every day?

Create a folder on your computer and store images that go along with your ideas. Do you want to retire on the beach? Find beautiful sunset pictures or real estate listings. Start researching travel destinations and save your research. Turn your dreams into goals and work towards them every day.

Your inner narrative

If you think you can do a thing or think you can't do a thing, you're right. – Henry Ford

While positive thinking by itself is not enough to achieve your goals, it's the only way to get started and it will help you persevere during difficult times. How many successful people have you met that had a negative attitude? The path to success in anything starts with the belief that it's possible, and the unwillingness to settle for less.

The inspiration for positive thinking can come from many places, like seeing someone else accomplish what you want to do. "If they can do it, I can do it." This has inspired many people to do things that seemed impossible. Your success begins or ends in your own mind. We all have an inner dialogue that speaks to us all day, every day. This inner voice can be our worst enemy or our best friend; the choice is truly up to us.

An inner dialogue of negative thoughts will be toxic and self-destructive, because it will cause you to doubt what you previously thought was obvious or doable. It will poison you against your goals and your self-worth. It will keep you from acting when you need to. In short, it will make it impossible to live up to your full potential.

In contrast, an inner dialogue of positive thoughts will propel you to new heights. You will do things that you thought impossible, and you will realize your goals and achieve success. Having a positive inner dialogue will help you realize your dreams, and your optimism will be a positive force in the lives of those around you.

Having a positive outlook is just the beginning of achieving your goals, however. Your upbeat mindset must be empowered by your strong work ethic and your willingness to go the distance as a trader. Know that you will make mistakes, but that you will grow from them. Your inner voice should encourage this growth and nurture you during these times. When mistakes stop being negative and become life lessons, the only thing that separates you from success is time.

You have to be your own biggest fan and believe in your future. You should strive to give encouragement and support to your best friend, yourself.

Exercise:

Affirmations are powerful. The truth of the matter is that you are what you believe. Consistently reinforcing positive thoughts about yourself *will* change how you view yourself. It may take some time for your personal perceptions to change, so find a few minutes every morning to give yourself a pep-talk. Here are a few useful affirmations that you can start with---but don't be afraid to come up with your own, personal positive reinforcement.

-"If he can do it, I can do it."

-"The market is not currently conducive to my current strategy, and that is the cause of my losing streak."
-"I have done the work. I am a competent trader. I know what I am doing. Success will come."
-"I understand that losses are part of trading and are a normal business expense."
-"Hindsight is 20/20. All I can do is follow my trading plan."
-"I know if I grow and learn, trading success will come."
-"I am willing to do what it takes to be a successful trader."

The right positive inner dialogue doesn't guarantee your success as a trader, but a negative inner dialogue can almost guarantee your failure.

Filter out the noise

The signal is the truth. The noise is what distracts us from the truth. - Nate Silver

As a trader, you are dealing with two types of information, signals and noise. Signals are meaningful pieces of information that cause traders to take action when the odds are in their favor. Signals are things that traders look for; technical buy signals, sell signals, or psychological signals like the market going up on bad news or down on good news, for example.

The noise is all the price action, news, predictions, opinions, projections, and forecasts that add no value to your trading. Your ability to filter out the unnecessary and focus on the important things is what will keep you calm while other traders are suffering a psychological downtrend.

You have to identify what type of information is meaningful to you. What are your signals? If your trading is only done at the end of the day, then intra-day price action may just be noise for you. Talking heads on financial news networks are just noise for everyone. You should identify exactly what time frame of price data and technical signals you need in order to make your trading decisions, and then focus like a laser on only those things. Avoid anything that doesn't add value to your trading system.

Too much data, tick by tick price action, news, and fear mongers can stress a trader out with information overload. Too much information will lead to a paralysis by over analysis for many, especially new traders. In the financial markets, many pundits and financial networks love to find interesting facts about the current market price action in a historical context. While these factoids may be interesting, they can't be used to create trading signals. They are just fun facts and noise. More information is not what is useful, rather it's the mining and filtering of what has value that makes the difference.

The more you can focus on what matters and avoid noise, confusion, and stress, the better your odds of staying calm and becoming a profitable trader.

Exercise:

It can be difficult to filter out the noise. Here are some questions to ask yourself to help you separate meaningless information from important facts.

-Does this financial news network add any value to my trading?
-Am I better off watching every price tick all day, or should I set alerts when my price targets are reached?
-If I am a day trader, should I only trade the open and closing hours instead of taking part all day?
-If I use end of day signals should I watch intra-day price action?
-Which people on social media add value to my trading and which add unnecessary noise?

-The only thing that should matter to you as a trader is actionable information, signal creation, and what has the potential to make you money. Find out what makes you money and focus on that stream of information.

Your time, money, and energy are your most important assets, spend them wisely.

Diversify your life

Trading can be your passion and a way to create wealth, but it's not the meaning of life. Your highest goal should be happiness, and trading should just be a stepping stone on the path to get you there. – Steve Burns

The best traders I know are not chained to their trading desks 24 hours a day, watching every tick, and obsessing over every market move. Being a trading workaholic is not the path to success; it's the path to burn out. Greater effort does not always mean better results. It's doing the right thing, at the right time, in the right way that creates results.

It's not healthy to work on your trading so much that it hurts your health, mindset, marriage, or friendships. While getting over the learning curve will require a lot of reading and research, even this difficult part of your journey must be balanced with the other areas of your life.

Becoming obsessed with trading can cause a loss of perspective. Losing trades take on too much meaning, and drawdowns can affect your self-worth. When you diversify your life with friends and family, hobbies, entertainment, healthy eating, and exercise, losing trades won't seem so bad. When a healthy trader has a losing trade, a losing week, or a losing month they can still fall back on the fact that they are happy, and have family and friends that care about them.

A support system is necessary to help keep a trader grounded and maintain the proper perspective about wins and losses. While the reasons for losses and losing streaks have to be analyzed so the trader can make adjustments, the emotional pain and negative self-talk can be minimized with a good support network.

Exercise:

Trading is hard, but it's important to take time to live a good life. Here are areas that will create mental balance and encourage a happy, healthy trading lifestyle.

-Maintain healthy eating habits and exercise regularly.
-Have a weekly date night with your significant other.
-Spend quality time with your children every day.
-Visit extended family on holidays.
-Maintain a healthy spiritual life through prayer or meditation.
-Enjoy a hobby that you love or find a new one.
-Relax and read a great book
-Volunteer or find a way to give back to your community

Remember why you started trading to begin with. You started trading to have a better life, not a worse one. When it's time to work then do your work, but when it's time to relax, then do that. A happy trader is more likely to be successful in all areas of life.

Managing uncertainty

Speculation is dealing with the uncertain conditions of the unknown future. Every human action is a speculation in that it's embedded in the flux of time. — Ludwig von Mises

We must accept the randomness of our short term results, and understand our long term edge to stay calm in the face of uncertainty. Traders are entrepreneurs. They don't trade for a regular paycheck, but they exchange that uncertainty for the potential of unlimited profits. New traders have a difficult time coming to grips with the uncertainty of the markets. It's hard for them to accept short term losses on the path to long term profitability. There are no guarantees in trading, only probabilities and possibilities. The more unknowns you can remove from your trading, the lower your stress level will be.

One of the most powerful things a trader can do to become calm is to limit their losses on a single trade. This is accomplished by limiting any one trade's position size, and having a stop loss in place. Buying option contracts in place of stock eliminates the possibility of losses larger than the option price. Traders that sell options should always have a hedge in place, using a long option to cap the size of a loss. By limiting your open trade positions and total capital at risk, you remove much of the uncertainty.

Since you can never be certain about what the market will do, you must turn your attention to what *you* will do. Traders have to have confidence that they will follow their system and plan. The financial dangers of going off your trading plan and position sizing parameters are not just financial, but also mental and emotional. While it's possible to trade the uncertainty of the markets price action, if you're uncertain about what you will do in response to that price action, you won't make it.

A profitable trader's confidence is not in the fact that they know what will happen next, the confidence is in knowing that they will respond to the market's action within the parameters of their profitable trading system, in a disciplined way.

Hall of Fame baseball players have more strikeouts than home runs. The ability for star athletes to experience the uncertainty of each at-bat without losing their confidence in their training and process, is what makes them win in the end. Just like in sports, traders with the ability to manage the mind will set themselves up for long term success.

One of the greatest life skills a person can possess is learning from losses instead of quitting. Growing your enthusiasm instead of shrinking from negativity will allow you to see yourself, the markets, and the world differently. Market environments shift quickly. They can go from range bound to trending. Prices can go from volatile to little movement. Short term results can be random; it's the disciplined, long term execution of a trading system with an edge that will lead to a winning career.

Great traders are profitable because they have become masters at managing uncertainty. They don't win because they can see the future, they win because they are certain of what they will do, in the present moment, when faced with uncertainty.

Exercise:

Managing uncertainty is critical to your success as a trader, and a big part of that will be being able to realize that stressful things will happen, but you will survive. This exercise will help you overcome your fear of the unknown.

First, find somewhere quiet where you can be alone with your thoughts. Make sure you are comfortable, and take a few minutes to just relax and slow your breathing and your thoughts. If a specific trading fear or worry starts tugging at your thoughts, then you can address it with this exercise. If not, just pick an imaginary scenario that you think could cause you stress.

Think about the worst thing that could happen to you during *one* trading day. Don't string days or weeks together, just focus on one trading day. What do you see happening? Is it a black swan event, something that you couldn't see coming, something no one predicted? You can't get into your brokerage account because all the servers have crashed? What is the WORST thing that can happen to you at that moment? If you are trading with a plan, with proper position sizing and risk management, you shouldn't have much to worry about. Even if you take a loss, it won't be a big one.

Remember that if you trade your plan, you will be fine every time, no matter what happens. When you deviate from your plan, you will put stress on yourself because you know you are putting yourself at risk, and if an unforeseen catastrophic event occurs, you will likely suffer mentally and financially.

Hindsight is a parasite

Hindsight is one of the worst trading tools. We trade based on current reality. Woulda, shoulda, coulda, are for traders with time machines. – Steve Burns

How do you stop trading with regret and hindsight? Focus on the present, and stay true to your trading plan. Hindsight can only teach lessons, it's a waste of time to use it for second guessing what you should have done. If you are trading your plan based on your system, your actions are based on discipline.

If you are following your plan, then you should have no regrets. You might have ideas on how to tweak your system for better entries or exits, for example, but you won't dwell on what could have happened. If you didn't follow your trading plan, then you may have some regret about a loss of discipline that caused you to not take an entry, exit, or not trade with the right position sizing. The only regret a trader should carry is for a loss of discipline.

You can get bitter or you can get better. Focus on what you can do to improve your future behavior. Learn where your weaknesses are and work hard to improve them. Stop repeating the same mistakes over and over again. When you learn your weaknesses and dedicate yourself to improvement, you will end the trend of bad trading habits and your better decisions result in trading success.

Consider hindsight to be a classroom, and spend your energy trading current market action. You may not be aware that you are making some of the same mistakes over and over again, and that is where your trading journal comes in. If you have been recording your feelings when you get in and out of trades, as well as your results, you will begin to see patterns emerge. Don't ignore these patterns, act on them. You can change your future as long as you are willing to let go of your past.

Change the channel from your own Personal History Channel to Current News. You can't relive the past, all you can do is learn from it.

Exercise:

Letting go of the past and forgiving yourself for your mistakes may sound easy, but if you're a trader that has made costly mistakes, placed stress on yourself and/or loved ones, or have become afraid to trade based on your past choices, this can be a difficult exercise.

Make a list of everything that you feel you have done wrong in the past year. You can add things that happened in the distant past, but you may want to start with one year to make sure you remember it well enough, and the feelings are still fresh. You can also include personal things if they affected your trading, or your trading affected your personal life in some way.

Spend some time with this list, referring to your trading plan and trading journal, to record every missed opportunity and perceived failure that you experienced. When you're ready, go through each item on the list and repeat:

I forgive myself
I'm still growing as a trader
I'll do better the next time
I'm sorry

It seems like a small thing, but the power of self-forgiveness is powerful. If you embrace this exercise, you will overcome some mental blockages that may be holding you back, and you will undoubtedly feel better about yourself and your future.

Angry trader, broke trader

If trading (or any other job or endeavor) is a source of anxiety, fear, frustration, depression, or anger, something is wrong—even if you are successful in a conventional sense. – Jack D. Schwager

Anger is our bodyguard that protects us from harm. Anger can propel us to right wrongs and defend ourselves, but it can also be a negative force. If a trader believes that the market action is out to get them, or that those high frequency traders and market makers are the ones causing them to be unprofitable, then they are headed down a bad road.

The market doesn't know we exist. The market as an entity doesn't exist. The stock market is a composite of all the buyers and sellers taking action simultaneously, and the current price is the reality of that intersection. Each trader has the freedom to dip their own bucket in the fast moving river of prices and try to drink from it. No traders are forced to buy or sell; they can choose their timing for entries and exits along with their trade size. It's truly the world's greatest free market.

You are punished or rewarded based on the quality of decisions you make. There is nothing to be angry about. If you are a low frequency trader, then high frequency traders can do little to affect you. If you are a swing trader, day traders are of little concern. If you are a trend follower, you have risen above the majority of the market noise and are just going with the flow of capital. The more you can limit your frustration as a trader, the happier and more profitable you will become.

A trader can also become angry with themselves based on past actions. It's just as destructive to turn your anger inward as it's to blame others. Being upset with yourself based on past mistakes makes it more difficult to come back from future challenges. And inevitably, your frustrations will spill out and affect your friends and family.

Trading small is the best way to manage anger, because this is generally a side effect of stress, and usually associated with a large loss. Accepting that the market is not out to get you is another cure for anger. All the other market participants put their own capital on the line and take risks, just like you do. If they win and we lose, then we need to be good sports about it and try again another day.

Revenge trading is a desperate attempt to force the market to give back money that was previously lost. Anger is one of the worst trading signals to use, and a trading plan can be the best protection against making angry trades. Trade the plan and not the anger.

Anger can be managed through acceptance and perspective. We must define who or what our enemy is. Is our anger justified based on reality, or is it just a loss of perspective? What is the most constructive thing that we can do to manage our anger? Is our decision on how to handle our anger going to get us closer to our goals?

Exercise:

Like the last exercise, this one is not always an easy one to do. It can be liberating to let go of the anger and contempt that we have been holding onto, and forgive people and entities that we feel have wronged us.

Make a list of everyone and everything that you feel have wronged you in the last year. Again, you can extend this out longer than a year. Spend some time with this list, and try to think about anyone or anything that influenced your trading in a challenging way, or any event that you found yourself being defensive or angry about. When you're ready, go through each item on the list and repeat:

I forgive you
You are not the reason that I have struggled
I make my own success

Anger is a part of being human. What matters is how we handle those feelings, and if we can create something positive from them. Rich traders are good at managing their feelings and their anger doesn't control their actions. Angry traders are quickly broke traders.

Letting go of ego

When I was able to separate my ego needs from making money, when I was able to accept being wrong. Before, admitting I was wrong was more upsetting than losing the money. I used to try to will things to happen. I figured it out, therefore it can't be wrong. When I became a winner, I said, "I figured it out, but if I'm wrong, I'm getting the hell out, because I want to save my money and go on to the next trade." By living the philosophy that my winners are always in front of me, it's not so painful to take a loss. – Marty Schwartz

An ego can be a healthy thing because it provides a trader with the self-confidence necessary to execute trades and be successful. A healthy ego understands a person's limitations and has a realistic assessment of their abilities. A trader with a healthy ego takes their trading seriously, but doesn't take themselves too seriously. Unfortunately, ego can also be the most destructive thing that a trader has to deal with because it has an aversion to risk and being wrong.

An unhealthy ego needs to be right, so it balks at taking a stop loss and holds onto a loser instead of cutting losses. The desire to never fail makes the ego want to look good to the outside world, no matter what. Making money becomes secondary to keeping up appearances. A trader with ego challenges tends to trade too big a position size and ignore risk management. The desire to make money has to override the need to be right about specific trades.

The longer you trade and the bigger your account grows, the more critical it will be for you to control your ego. Often, a trader will learn about his ego when he has a losing streak. How you handle a losing streak will give you a glimpse into your future success. Ego management determines success as much as a robust trading system and commitment to risk management. An unchecked ego can destroy your account before you know what hit you.

Keep your ego in check by using a trading system, risk management, and follow your trading plan regardless of how you feel. Spend time getting to know what motivates you, especially in times of stress.

Exercise:

Our ego is an important part of who we are. Without ego, we wouldn't do very well. It keeps us secure and it helps us flourish. In order to maintain a healthy relationship with it, it's important that we show our ego the respect it deserves, while keeping it within the boundaries that are necessary for our personal and professional success.

In this exercise, focus on developing a relationship with your ego by having a conversation. Acknowledge that your ego is a powerful and useful part of you, but that it has some limitations that it may not be aware of. Your conversation with your ego may look something like this.

I value our relationship, and know that you are an important part of my life. I know that without you, I could easily find myself in danger, and I know that I need you to help me identify

threats to my safety. But I also know that there are areas in my life that you don't fully understand. I promise that I won't take unnecessary risks, but I would like you to try to trust that there is more to us than just avoiding risks and being right. I may make mistakes, but I am making them with the best intentions, and I will learn from them.

Developing a relationship with your ego, acknowledging when things are getting out of hand, and being able to refocus on your trading plan, risk management, and robust trading system will give you a trading edge.

That cotton trade was almost the deal breaker for me. It was at that point that I said, 'Mr. Stupid, why risk everything on one trade? Why not make your life a pursuit of happiness rather than pain?' – Paul Tudor Jones

If you want to make it as a trader, you must manage your exposure to mental, emotional, and financial pain. The good news is, you have control over your pain level through your decision making process. It's important to understand what your limits are so you know what you can withstand. What size loss can you handle without wanting to hurl? How volatile does a market have to get to keep you up at night? Can you handle the emotional ups and downs of day trading?

If you trade the right position size, trading can be a lot of fun, but if you trade too large, it can quickly become a nightmare. You have to find the type of trading that is right for you. Your search is for the time frame, trading vehicle, volatility, leverage, speed, and position size that fit your personality and stress tolerance.

You won't make it as a trader if you spend your days hurting mentally, emotionally, or even physically. Your trading regimen should be a process that protects you from any form of misery. The best way to guarantee that you won't be an unhappy trader, is to spend the time developing your own trading philosophy. It should be well researched, including backtesting and chart studies, so you know the risks and the worst case scenario. Your worst case scenarios should be something you can handle, and not something that will cause you duress.

Strive to make your worst possible day, a 3% drawdown in total trading capital by limiting your risk to three trades with a stop loss and position sizing structured so if all three trades go against you, you are down 3% on one day. Based on the quality of the market environment, you may opt to have one, two, or even no open positions. Your primary focus is on survival and profitability is second. You won't make any money if your trading becomes so painful that you quit.

Your risk of mental ruin is a real threat to your trading success. You can come back from financial losses, but it's difficult to come back from a blow to your confidence. When you sit down at your trading desk in the morning and realize you are already stressed, you're already in trouble. Protect against traumatic events by trading small and guarding your capital. Your greatest asset is your well-being, protect it at all costs.

Exercise:

Here is a list of ways that you can avoid experiencing painful losses. Study this list and add your own, personalized methods for staying safe.
You need to trade small, meaningful positions.

-Don't fight a trend.

-Honor your first stop loss.
-Limit your total risk exposure.
-Don't hold and hope, cut and run.
-Trade in your comfort zone.
-Don't use leverage that is stressful for you.
-Don't trade markets you don't understand.
-Go to cash if the market becomes too stressful.
-Trade smaller during losing streaks.
-Listen to your trading plan.

The less pain your expose yourself to, the easier it will be to stay calm and be a profitable trader.

Losing and staying calm

If I have positions going against me, I get right out; if they are going for me, I keep them... If you have a losing position that is making you uncomfortable, the solution is very simple: Get out, because you can always get back in. – Paul Tudor Jones

Winning trades will do little to test you. When your biggest problem is to let your winner run, take your profits now, or use a trailing stop to lock in profits, you won't have much to worry about. It's the losing trades that will test your nerves, confidence, and ability to stay calm in the middle of the market's price action. The way you handle a losing trade will set the standard for future, stressful trades. There are two aspects to managing losing trades: time and money.

Limit your exposure to losing trades and stay in winning trades for as long as possible. Depending on your time frame, a losing trade may last a day and a winning trade could last weeks or a month. A day trader's losing trade may last a few minutes, while a winning trade could last for hours. This is what is meant by letting your winners run and cutting your losers short. Guard your time by cutting losses and looking for other trading opportunities.

The other aspect that should be a primary focus is managing financial loss. The best way to stay calm while losing money is to lose as little as possible. Sounds simple, but if you are trading too large, you will eventually have a loss that may be difficult to recover from. Most traders can handle losing ½% or 1% of their trading capital if they're wrong because this causes little emotional or financial stress. More aggressive traders with high win rates may choose to go as high as 2% of their total trading capital.

Remember that this is not referring to position sizing, it's referring to your stop loss being hit. If you are trading with $50,000, then 1% is $500 of your trading capital. If you are trading a $50 priced stock and the key chart support is at $48, you can trade 250 shares and stopping out at $48 would be a $500 loss, or 1% of total trading capital.

Exercise:

Acknowledge that losing streaks and drawdowns in capital will quickly unnerve you and you should avoid them as much as possible. Study this list and add to it when you experience other examples of losing streaks and drawdowns. The more you learn from your losses, the more you will be able to avoid them.

Trend fighting: Buying stocks when a market is in a downtrend will lead to multiple losses. Momentum strategies and support buying strategies will fail. It's not the strategies, it's the market environment.

Trend trading in a range bound market: You can't profit from trends when there are none. When a market is inside a range of price support and resistance, higher highs and lower lows are rejected, which gives the trend trader no profits. Trend traders using breakout signals will be stopped out, which leads to multiple losses as price returns to the trading range.

You're zigging while the market is zagging: A trader can get out of sync with a market. They can be stopped out of a long position before it rallies and get left on the sidelines. Or a trader can wait to buy a dip to a support level as price comes close to the buy point, when it suddenly reverses and rallies, leaving the trader empty handed.

Your ability to stay calm in the markets will largely be determined by how good you are at managing losses. Limit the time and money spent losing, and you will increase your ability to win and make money. Lose fast, win slow, and move on to the next opportunity. But most of all, stay calm and trade on.

Happy trader, rich trader

I feel my success comes from my love of the markets. I am not a casual trader. It's my life. I have a passion for trading. It's not merely a hobby or even a career choice for me. There is no question that this is what I am supposed to do with my life. – Ed Seykota

The best traders are those that truly love what they do. To be successful, you have to love the game, you need to be excited by the uncertainty, and you should be energized by the opportunity. Loving to trade will create the passion needed do the hard work and overcome adversity. Learning to trade is difficult and time consuming. It takes time to acquire the skills necessary to be profitable. Traders looking for a quick fix will likely watch as their money is handed over to traders focusing on long term capital growth.

Trading is your opportunity to outsmart, out trade, and out last other market participants. If you are committed to trading the right way, you may find trading to be the best job that you ever have. It's flexible, with traders working both part-time and full-time in the field. Trading can be done either full time as a living, part time as a passion, or for capital appreciation for building a nest egg. The most important thing to remember is that you must do what is best for you and your lifestyle.

Trading for a living with a small account will not be much fun, and trading for rent month after month is a recipe for disaster. You need to have a good quality of life, and that requires being set up properly, with the right amount of capital to accomplish your goals, and a safety net in case things go wrong.

You need to understand where you are in your trading journey. Don't try to speed up your learning curve. The market will still be there when you're ready to trade real money, trade for a living, or trade with a bigger account size. Stay with the level that makes you happy and advance to the next stage when you're ready to grow. Trying to trade before you are ready is the fast track to stress and unhappiness.

As you develop as a trader, your #1 goal should be happiness. The easiest way to be happy in the markets is to be profitable. But even when you lose money, you need to accept that it's just part of the game, and start looking forward to your next chance to win. If you are energized during your research and trading, then you will stay happy. Do more of what you like and less of what you don't like. The things that traders dislike are big losses, holding a losing trade, drawdowns, and a loss of discipline. The solution to these problems is to follow your trading plan, no matter what.

It's much easier to be calm when you are happy. Create a trading process that you like and trade inside a lifestyle that brings you joy. Filter your trading decisions through the question of "Will this make me happy?"

Exercise:

It's important to keep things in perspective. It's easy to get caught up in the day-to-day activities of life and of trading, and forget that there is a reason we are working so hard. Anytime you find yourself feeling lost or unsure of why you are doing what you're doing, make a list of the 50 things that make you happy. Put a date on it and save it. Your answers will change every time you do the exercise, and you may find interesting patterns or simple truths that will lead you to a new, happier place.

As a trader, your goal is not only trade, but to reap the rewards that trading brings: fun, time, financial freedom, and independence. Your trading journey should take you to your ultimate goal, happiness.

Conclusion

I would tell that trader to think of each trade as one of the next one thousand he's going to make. If you start thinking in terms of the next one thousand trades, all of a sudden you've made any single trade seem very inconsequential. Who cares if a particular trade is a winner or a loser? It's just another trade. – Tom Basso

Traders that are emotionally calm and approach trading as a business, have better odds of profitability than the thrill seekers and gamblers that come to the market. 1/3 of trading is based on logic, and 2/3 is based on emotions. Your trading system is the needed logic that filters the market's price action. Your trading plan is your anchor.

10 things that a trader has to overcome to stay calm and be profitable.

Impulsiveness-Replace impulsiveness with proven rules that filter emotions into the correct actions.
Impatience-Replace market noise and emotions with quantified entries and exits based on signals.
Anger-Replace animosity towards the market with respect for price action and emotionless trading.
Uncertainty-Accept the randomness of short term results and embrace the long term edge.
Laziness-Reduce stress by doing homework when the market is closed so you can be ready when the market is open.
Greed-Replace the need for immediate wins with a process for consistently growing capital.
Fear-Replace your fear of failure with confidence in your system and your ability to follow it successfully.
Ego-Replace your need to be right about specific trades with the desire to make money.
Hope-Replace the hope that a losing trade will recover with a well-planned stop loss.
Stress-Reduce stress by choosing to have small losses fast instead of big, slow losses.

Profitable traders are rarely overstressed. Emotions are natural, they're part of being human. It's the way we manage them that makes the difference. The egomaniacs and the gamblers are usually the ones that lose it all. A good trader is a business person and not a gambler. They see risks and rewards, profits and losses, divorced from their egos and emotions. The calm traders are the ones that keep a level head and maximize opportunities when the market presents them. They have mastered the art of being patient, trading small, staying calm, and trading profitability.

Are you a calm trader?

Be a better trader

In the New Trader 101 e-course, you'll get:
-13 high quality videos covering how and why to trade
-Real trade examples with detailed charts
-An active member forum with hundreds of ongoing conversations
Visit New Trader 101 and join other traders just like you!

Did you enjoy this eBook?
Please consider writing a review.

Read more of our bestselling titles:
New Trader 101
Moving Averages 101
Trading Habits

49484026R00022

Made in the USA
San Bernardino, CA
25 May 2017